Your School Day

Dona Herweck Rice

Going to School

walking

biking

riding in a bus

crossing the street

riding in a car

Greeting People

Morning Routines

schedule

announcements

discussion

collect homework

Pledge of Allegiance

Reading

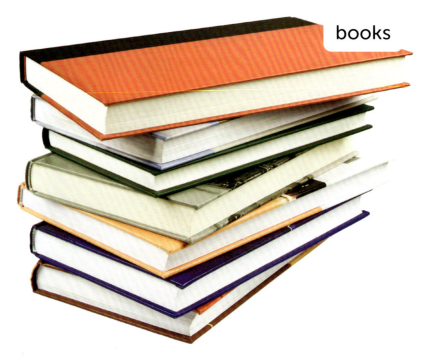

books

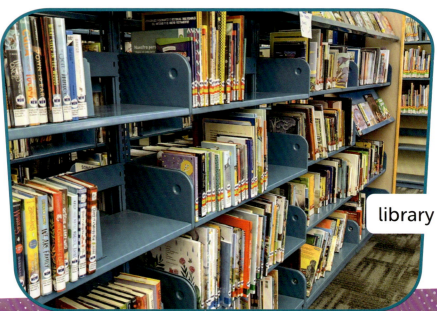

library

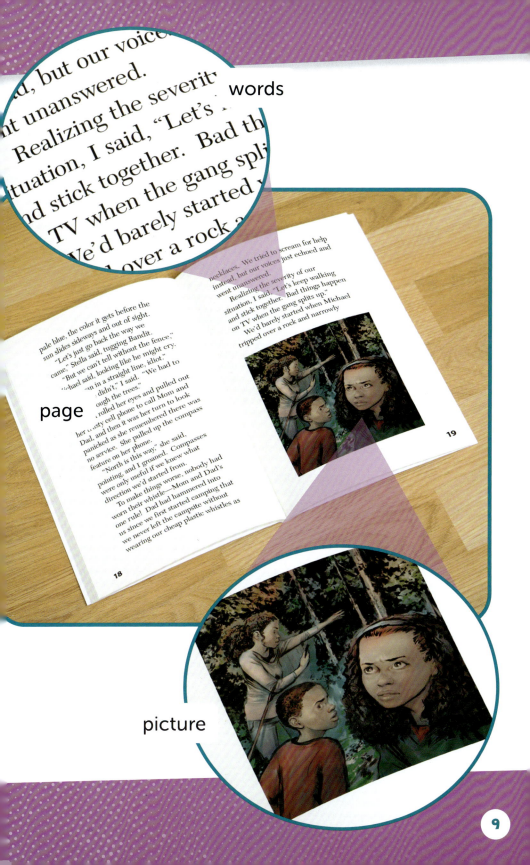

words

page

picture

Subjects

language arts

math

10

science

social studies

physical education (PE)

Recess

run

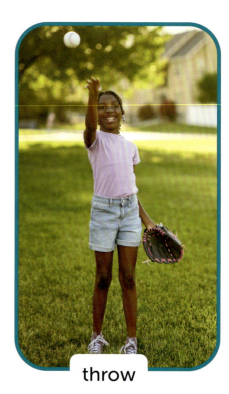
throw

jump rope

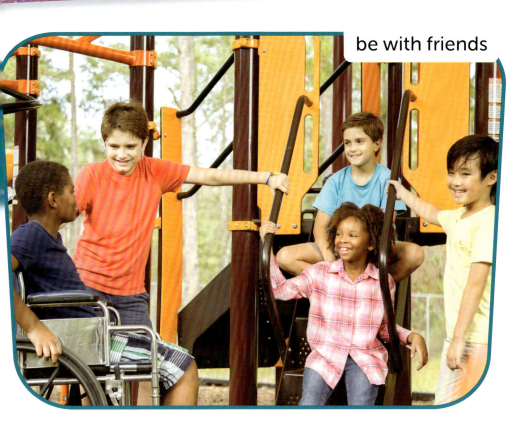

be with friends

equipment

Learning Groups

independent

partners

small group

class

assembly

Lunchtime

eat

drink

sit down

clean up

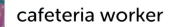
cafeteria worker

Important People

custodian

principal

librarian

Important Places

classroom

playground

School Equipment

desk and chair

table and chairs

computer

bulletin board

board

Rules to Know

line up

listen

Going Home

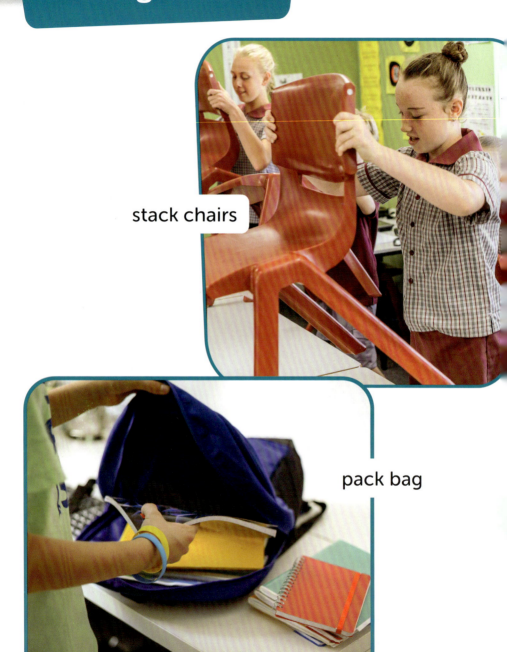

stack chairs

pack bag

say goodbye

leave

do homework

Consultants
Janessa Lang, M.A. Ed.
Elementary Teacher, Los Angeles

Publishing Credits
Rachelle Cracchiolo, M.S.Ed., *Publisher*
Emily R. Smith, M.A.Ed., *SVP of Content Development*
Véronique Bos, *VP of Creative*
Jill Malcolm, *Senior Graphic Designer*

Image Credits: p.15 Shutterstock/PhotoRK; all images from iStock, Shutterstock, or in the public domain

Library of Congress Control Number available upon request.

This book may not be reproduced or distributed in any way without prior written consent from the publisher.

5482 Argosy Avenue
Huntington Beach, CA 92649
www.tcmpub.com
ISBN 979-8-3309-0483-9
© 2025 Teacher Created Materials, Inc.
Printed by: 51497
Printed in: China